This book is dedicated to the person who has pushed me to achieve heights I had never imagined. De'Antwaine Moye, you are one of the most gifted minds on this earth. Anyone given the opportunity to sit with you is in the presence of greatness. Thank you for obeying God and showing me and countless others a version of our assignments that would've been undiscovered without your prompting. Keep being a midwife to the Kingdom's greatest minds.

PROCEED

A DEVOTIONAL FOR *NERVOUS* LEADERS

JAMES MCCARROLL

IMPACTFUL
publishing
Murfreesboro, TN

Published by Impactful Publishing, a Division of Holy Impact Publishing, LLC

PO Box 11055 – Murfreesboro, TN 37130, USA

ISBN: 978-1-7353255-3-8

For more information, address: holyimpactmovment@gmail.com

Cover Design: James McCarroll

Book Design: Soumi Goswami
               soumi.goswami.pub@gmail.com

Book Editor: Marla Larkin
               Mlarkin2@yahoo.com

Copy Editor and Proofreader: Mary Neretlis

To contact James McCarroll send an email to:

engagements@jamesmccarroll.org

For other works by this author, visit: Jamesmccarroll.org

Printed in the United States of America

Table of Contents

Introduction

As I write this introduction, I am on a flight returning to Nashville, leaving a conference in St. Thomas, USVI. Each morning during my trip this past week, I got up at sunrise to go and sit on the beach of Sapphire Bay. There I spent several hours taking inventory of my life and ministry. I revisited the mental images of the events of years gone by. A smile grew over my face as I recalled the successes of life and ministry. But simultaneously, I also winced at the remembrance of life's disappointments and shortfalls. Needless to say, every morning was a roller coaster of emotions.

Then came the most difficult space of reflection, *the echoes of unpursued callings.* I sat and thought about the book concepts, which still remain housed on the shelves of my mind. I revisited the accomplishments and assignments, for which I gave myself a grade of "incomplete." As the water teased the shore with its temporary advances, creating a symphony of sound to serve as a soundtrack to my time of introspection, I realized at the root of every unfulfilled assignment was a sense of nervousness and trepidation, causing me to get stuck at the starting line.

Heaven's starting pistol sounded, but for whatever reason, I didn't – or wouldn't – move. Maybe it was uncertainty of the future or possibly even the fear of success; either way, my progress was relatively nonexistent.

Flying home, I began to grasp the gravity of callings deferred. It is much deeper than not writing a book or composing a song. In the greater plan of God, when a calling goes unanswered, we may be refusing to build the bridge God planned to use to help others make it to their destiny. If the ministry isn't birthed, the victim of domestic violence will have no safe haven. If the book isn't written, the depressed teenager may die an untimely death because there was no voice to escort them from the space of suicidal thoughts. I think you get my point. *Deferred callings usually prolong redemptive movements.*

So, this book is really not about you. It's about the hundreds of lives who wait on you to say "yes" to the calling of God and move forward to it. You are the answer sent by heaven in response to the prayers of those needing a way out. This book is simply a tool to call you from the sidelines and onto the field for the "big play." It's time for you to stop choosing to spend life in "park" and make a decision to proceed.

This work is not intended to be lengthy because every moment you are on the sidelines, Satan is gaining more ground. The goal of this devotional is to get to the root of what is causing you to be stuck and help you discover the freedom that will position you to carry out the assignment that lies ahead. As you complete this devotional, I provide several suggestions to assist you in optimizing its effectiveness as follows:

Find an uninterrupted space.

This process requires deep, concentrated introspection. Therefore, find a space that has few to no distractions. I recommend taking a personal retreat where you can control what gains access to the room where you read and reflect. This will ensure you can hear from God and yourself as clearly as possible.

Take down your "walls."

Your greatest opponent in this process will be you. Your doubts, fears and presuppositions become stumbling blocks to your ability to hear God with accuracy and trust yourself enough to engage in the hard conversations. Make a covenant with yourself to not attempt to prove your worth or correctness, but rather allow yourself to be "naked and unashamed" before the inspecting gaze of heaven.

Be transparent and authentic.

Significant growth and transformation happen when we bring our honest and authentic selves to the moment of hard conversation. Understand that even the worst parts of your life and character are just as valuable in whom you have become as your best parts. Therefore, don't approach this space with a mask or in partial honesty. Be fully present and give the LORD and His calling access to all of you.

Take off the "straight-jacket" of your possibility.

God can only take our lives as far as we give ourselves permission to go. As you go through this journey to gain courage, refuse to limit God by lowering the ceiling of your potential. Give the LORD permission to set the height, depth and breadth of your life's purpose and possibility. You will soon discover God has more in store for you than you could have ever imagined.

Adopt God's truth as your own.

Change begins the moment we allow the truth of God to move from a concept in our heads to becoming the truth in our hearts. As you begin to hear the revelations and insights the LORD has for your life, accept and adopt them as your own. As you hear them, give yourself permission to become a tangible manifestation of the holy insight you've received. Before you know it, what you've heard will become what you witness as your soul's reality.

Now, let's begin the conversation.

NERVOUSNESS IS NORMAL

Have you ever felt as if God mailed the invitation to the assignment to the wrong address? After years of training ministers and working with leaders, I have discovered one's calling can so outweigh our perceptions of who we are that it is not uncommon to question whether or not we are the person for the job. It is usually because God's timing for introducing the calling doesn't seem to match our maturity, competence or emotional readiness to pursue or accomplish it with any expectation of success. Such an experience can bring a sense of nervousness. According to Healthline, "Nervousness is a natural response to a stressful event. It's temporary and resolves once the stress has passed...It is a perfectly natural response to a new experience or situation that's outside of your comfort zone" (Santos-Longhurst, 2019). In short, sometimes the calling of God can cause us to have "nerves."

A *LinkedIn* report found 80 percent of working professionals experience nerves when they start a new job. (Seaver, 2020) The article states the most nerve-wracking concern (according to 55 percent of those asked) is a general worry they won't be good at their job quickly enough. Secondly, is they won't ever succeed. Though there are other concerns such as social impressions or lack of qualifications, I think the first two are more than sufficient reasons, which many leaders can relate to.

I don't know about you, but when God presents an assignment, it seems to highlight my inadequacies more than my potential. My knee-jerk reaction is to say to myself, "There is no way I can do this." It is usually at this point when motivational speakers and preachers make statements like, "God will never give you a vision that you can't accomplish without Him" or, "God is calling you because you are stronger than you realize." Though these sentiments do provide some theological insight and emotional "push," they don't magically eliminate the jitters with my expectation of the magnitude of what's ahead.

When it's big, sometimes it just *feels* big. God never intended for us to negate the enormity of the callings, nor "psyche ourselves out" in an attempt to minimize the calling to an intellectually-manageable level. God presents it to us knowing it will make us nervous. God knows it is beyond us and the sheer thought of God's ask is enough to make us resign immediately. In essence, God is aware – and most likely certain – that the assignment will make us nervous. But let me assure you, our nervousness is not unholy; it is simply human. God is not offended that His thoughts and ways prove to be above ours. That's what it means to be "God."

So, if you are nervous about the new assignment, you are in great company. Most of the biblical leaders were nervous when they were called. Moses couldn't believe

God would give him the role of a national spokesman when he clearly had a speaking deficiency. Gideon felt inadequate. Peter felt too sinful. Isaiah felt too profane. Paul felt unworthy. But they were all called.

And nervous.

After all, it isn't the nervousness that is unholy. Our nervousness becomes unholy when we allow our sense of inadequacy to be used as a valid reason to not proceed in the assignment that has been placed before us. When we justify our paralysis or unwillingness to answer the calling of God, in essence, we say to God, "Your will is not going to be done if it doesn't fit my perception of who I am and what I can do." Such an act of blatant defiance is never an acceptable response to the summons of God.

You see, the calling doesn't come to you based on the knowledge of your nervousness. It comes to you based on the hope of your compliance with the plan of God. However, God knows your willingness to heed the call will require some inner wrestling with fears, doubts and self-imposed limitations.

Thus, God not only gives the general invitation, but also couples it with the motivation needed for us to find the inner fortitude to take a chance and move forward. Whether it is through others sent to affirm the calling (like Ananias) or miraculous signs (like Gideon's fleece), God will make every effort to confirm the calling in a way that allows you to have peace to proceed.

The book of Joshua is more than just a book about the nation of Israel conquering the land of Canaan. It is written to give us a preview of life on the other side of nervousness. It is written to show us that, like Joshua, our courage and obedience on the other side of our personal fears will not leave us underwhelmed and empty-handed. If we are willing to be nervous *and* keep moving forward, we will soon discover God didn't make a mistake in choosing us. Instead, the invitation is the starting point of a journey of grace, strategy and power that will position us to see growth, miracles and success, and which will defy our imagination. Joshua shows us that it's okay to be nervous.

Just be nervous *and* proceed.

Have you allowed your nervousness to cripple you? What does that say about your perception of self? What does it say about your perception of the assignment? What does it say about your perception of God?

What if any negative perception was wrong? How would you move forward?

YOU ARE MADE FOR THIS MOMENT!

After the death of Moses the servant of the Lord,
the Lord spoke to Joshua son of Nun, Moses' assistant,
saying, "My servant Moses is dead. Now proceed to
cross the Jordan, you and all this people, into the land
that I am giving to them, to the Israelites."

– Joshua 1:1-2 NRSV

It is always more comfortable to travel from the passenger's seat. There we experience the views of the driver without any of the pressures involved in navigating the road. This is most likely how Joshua felt. He was able to experience the private conversations on Mt. Sinai. He was given access to spaces of fellowship and communion with the greatest prophet in the history of Israel. Then it happened. Moses died. Though Joshua knew the day would eventually come, no one could have prepared him for that moment when he received the news and felt the cool chill of uncertainty and unreadiness that flooded his soul.

He was anointed for it and publicly appointed to it, but until the moment of Moses' death, it was but winsome rhetoric and distant reality. Now, the task of leading the greatest movement in his people's history was upon him. As he is in the "preparation room" of destiny, God takes a moment to speak to Joshua directly about what God plans to do through his life. In short, the LORD wanted Joshua to know this moment of leadership had

Joshua's name on it. No longer could he enjoy the trip from the passenger seat – it was now time to drive.

You purchased this journal for one of two reasons. Either you wanted to support the author (and for that I'm very grateful), or you are tired of sitting on the sidelines with dreams, aspirations, plans and conversations for which you are honestly too nervous to pursue. If you are in that second group, you know how it feels to be Joshua. You have wandered at the edge long enough and the LORD is "nudging" you to do what you have been set aside and called to accomplish.

The first thing you are going to have to do is own the fact that the calling has YOUR name on it. There has been no mistake. The assignment is not at the wrong address. YOU ARE THE PERSON FOR THIS TASK. Do you have issues? Yes. Are you fostering shortcomings and character flaws? Yes. But your name has still been identified by heaven, and the True and Living God is awaiting your RSVP. Not only is heaven waiting; those depending on you to guide their lives into a new stage of existence are also waiting. The unavoidable reality is this: you are made for this moment, and this moment is designed for YOU to be heaven's choice to bring it to pass.

THE UPGRADE:
SECURITY

If you have truly seen where the matter lies,
throw away the thought of how you might seem
to others, and be content if you live the rest
of your life in the manner that your nature wills.

– Marcus Aurelius, *Meditations*

Of all the character traits which determine the outcomes of our lives and journeys, none is more critical than personal security (or the lack thereof). How you view yourself does more than just determine your self-esteem. It is the primary basis from which your self-efficacy, self-achievement and personal success in every area of your life will be pursued. Many people never forge the path or tackle the obstacles before them because of how they have crafted the lens through which they see themselves. On the other hand, those with high levels of achievement clearly have a different sense of self-awareness that allows them to face life's challenges with a level of resolve and relentless confidence that fuels their certainty of the fact that if the opportunity found their address, then it must be possible for them to achieve.

If you look at your life closely, you will soon discover that your fears, not your hopes, have set the limit on what you have achieved and produced. Why does this happen? What is determining whether your fears or hopes respond to the assignment of God when it is introduced to you? It is simply centered on your self-awareness.

In his ground-breaking work, *Emotional Intelligence: Why It Can Matter More Than IQ*, Daniel Goleman defines self-awareness as "the ability to recognize and understand personal moods and emotions and drives, as well as their effect on others." (Goleman, 1995) The reason many leaders wrestle with being able to crack the ceiling of their low-level achievement is because they honestly don't know themselves – at least, not as it pertains to their responses to life's challenges. Their talent and work ethic has positioned them to be promoted by others, but their limited knowledge of self prevents them from pursuing previously unforeseen greatness when they have to achieve it for themselves.

To gain a greater understanding of why you have a hard time moving forward when great opportunities are before you, Goleman suggests that you have to gain an awareness of the emotional responses attached to various actions – or more importantly, reactions – when circumstances present themselves. It is learning to train your mind to be attentive to how and when your emotions swing, and subsequently analyze and discover the causes. Like most leaders, you probably recognize the fact that you are emotional. You can also recognize moments when your emotions are more or less positive. However, you can't quite understand why that happens, and even much less control it.

Usually, such emotions are brought about by the influence of others or life's encounters as it concerns their effect on how you view yourself. It could be hurtful things that were said in past moments of failure or disappointment that make you afraid to position yourself to possibly see those conversations re-experienced. It could be traumatic experiences that were the result of bold moves and how they produced a negative impact on your life or the lives of others, causing you to want to position yourself or those around you to not witness the hurt or revisit the events. Finally, there may have been traumatic encounters that blind-sided you when you stepped out of the conventional path and caused pain that scarred you in deep and long-lasting ways.

These outcomes are rehearsed every time you receive the invitation to great moments. As soon as you hear the summons to climb to the next peak of achievement, your palms get sweaty, your heart rate increases and you swiftly prepare the litany of reasons why it shouldn't be you.

That response ends today.

I want you to pay very close attention to the excuse you have been giving yourself for not becoming. You will notice that the moments given as reasons not to move forward are from earlier, less experienced versions of yourself. Upon close examination, you will discover that those moments were the classrooms where you grew from the version of yourself that had the experience to who you are now. And even if the voices are still real and could resurface, your existence in this moment is a reminder that you can live beyond the criticism, chants of failure and debasing jargon of onlookers. Not only can you live beyond it, you can thrive after it. Simply put, *God moves after the adversity.*

Knowing that greater outcomes are possible and success beyond imagination is awaiting you, you have a decision to make. You must now decide whether you will continue to re-cast yourself in the negative mental episodes of years gone by or rewrite the success narrative from which your faith will be born. Will you allow your past emotional defaults to rob you of the attainment of your God-given purpose, or will you rise above them to discover the heights to which you are being beckoned? Consider this excerpt from Hamlet:

Thou has been...
A man that Fortune's buffets and rewards
Has taken with equal thanks...Give me that man
That is not passion's slave, and I will wear him
In my heart's core, aye, in my heart of hearts
As I do thee...

Self-awareness awakens us to the reality of our potential to experience fluctuating emotions and end up as "passion's slave." It shows us that there are things in life that trigger responses and feelings that can guide us into a perpetual pause or re-route us from destiny to mediocrity. However, as Goleman identifies, to realize the greatness to which we are called, we must also learn self-mastery. This means that we have to be able to gain a sense of control that enables our purpose and calling to override our passions so that the plan of God is not threatened by the environments we may encounter on the journey of achievement. As Paul wrote to the church at Corinth, we must "bring into captivity every thought into the obedience of Christ." (2 Corinthians 10:5)

When you make the conscious decision to no longer trade great purpose for distrustful passions, a new door of achievement will open to you. You will discover that on the other side of fear, a land of opportunity is reserved to which you had been blinded the entire time. The mirage of failed outcomes will be seen as nothing more than a faint illusion designed to distract you from becoming what you were inevitably designed by God to be.

However, the greatest triumph will not be an external entity. It will be the achievement of gaining personal security. A self-awareness of your real potential and competence will take up new residence in your perception of self. You will gain the strength to know that you may have been the product of your past environments and acquaintances, but your future environments and acquaintances will be the product of your understanding of presence and purpose. For the first time, you will walk in a holy security of self that refuses to leave any part of your future to those around you but, instead, will make every effort to shape it to fit the plan and purpose of God's will for it. You will become settled in who you have been created, called and cultivated by God to be on the earth.

When you are secure in your purpose, you will no longer run from the invitations of heaven to pursue moments of unforeseen accomplishments. You will accept the assignment fully assured that it is at the right address and pre-destined for *your* life. Though there will be challenges, emotions, bumps and obstacles, you will rest assured that it was all factored into the equation before the calling was offered to you. And, besides, none of it has the capacity to prevent the plan of God from being successfully completed. It can only add to your character and sharpen you in the process. You are fully certain that the upcoming series of events will finally find you standing on the heap of great accomplishment as an indication to the world around you that YOU ARE THE ONE MADE FOR THIS MOMENT.

Winning the War Within:
You are Called and Qualified
(An exercise for reflection)

What about you makes you think you can't be the one God has called?

_____

_____

_____

_____

_____

_____

_____

What does God see in you that made him choose you?

_____

_____

_____

_____

_____

_____

_____

_____

In the following scriptures, which other bible characters doubted God's ability to use them? How did the LORD resolve their issue? Do you resonate with any of them? Why?

1. Exodus 4:10-17
2. Genesis 18:9-14
3. Judges 6:11-16

_____
_____
_____
_____
_____
_____

How does 2 Corinthians 12:9 speak to you about how the LORD can use you for His work, despite your shortcomings?

_____
_____
_____
_____
_____
_____

PROCEED

Statement of Affirmation:

I am made for this moment, and this moment is made for me.

Closing Prayer:

Heavenly Father, help me embrace the truth You have made me for this moment and assignment. Give me the grace needed to move forward in faith. In Jesus' name, I ask this, AMEN.

Hearing from the LORD
(THIRTY MINUTES OF SILENT REFLECTION):

What is the LORD saying about how you need to adjust your view of self before you begin this assignment?

_____

_____

_____

_____

_____

_____

_____

_____

_____

_____

_____

_____

_____

_____

_____

_____

_____

YOUR
NAME IS
ALREADY
ON IT

Every place that the sole of your foot will tread upon I have given to you, as I promised to Moses. From the wilderness and Lebanon as far as the great river, the river Euphrates, all the land of the Hittites, to the Great Sea in the west shall be your territory.

– Joshua 1:3-4 NRSV

One of the greatest enjoyments of going to dinner at certain restaurants is making a reservation. The only thing better is when others make the reservation for me. In the case of the latter, all that is required is to arrive and be guided by the host or hostess to a table, which has been designated specifically for our party. With reservations, the restaurant has already determined where we would dine; we only have to take action to make it a reality.

This is what the LORD was doing when He gave Joshua the details of the area designated for the Hebrew people. Heaven had made the pre-arrival reservation, but now it was time for Joshua to position the Israelites to take ownership. God had already gone before Joshua and secured the Promised Land. But Joshua needed to know his responsibility to bring it into Israelite possession.

God uses language in this scripture, which speaks to God's process for promised possession. He uses the phrases, "your foot *will tread* upon," "I *have given* to you," and *"shall be* your territory." It seems paradoxical to use two different tenses (future and past tense) to discuss the same acquisition.

When God speaks to you about the destination, it is usually after the divine transaction is resolved, even when you first hear of it. IF THE OUTCOME IS NOT FULLY SECURED, the LORD doesn't give the invitation to move forward. When the outcome is secured, you will not only get the urge; you will also get the details. Therefore, if you are receiving a solid urge to meet a specific place or outcome, it may be an indication that the LORD has already gone before you and finished the process so He can escort you to the possession. However, you still have to move forward to possess it.

THE**UPGRADE:**
ASSURANCE

*Turning your imagination loose may take some
practice…You may be so afraid of failure that
you dare to dream only within precise and restrictive
boundaries. You may be reluctant to set the bar
too high for fear that you couldn't possibly jump
over it. Yet, if truth be told, a [big] vision knows
no boundaries. It has massive resources at its disposal.*

– Bill Perkins, *Awaken the Leader Within*

The outcome is already determined before you received
the invitation.

God is not calling you, hoping that you will have what
it takes to make it happen. He's calling you because he
knows *He* will make it happen. However, many of us
wonder IF it can happen after being called. In short, we
lack certainty that God is really "God enough" to make
it happen with someone like us. Such a reality makes us
seek several other voices of affirmation and confirmation
before we make a move to fulfill the calling.

This hesitation is usually the result of the fact that *we
haven't seen it happen before.* God's calling on our lives
is usually so unique that it rests beyond the database of

"God accomplishments" in our lives. It's something that we haven't seen God do in the bible or in the lives of those around us, so we begin to second guess whether it is something that God even does.

We forget that every miracle from the creation of the world to opening blinded eyes had a debut on the earth. There was a time when the earth had never seen God do it, yet it was done anyway. This is no different. Elohim is still the God of creation and imagination. God can still set bushes on fire without consuming them and give healthy function to lame feet. But he can also create things that have yet to be seen and documented.

Your calling was on hold in heaven until this moment. It was still in the waiting room of miraculous manifestations that had yet to be released into the world. BUT IT'S ABOUT TO COME TO PASS. God is sending you a private invitation to the unveiling of His newest movement on the earth. Though we haven't seen it, we serve a God who specializes in the unseen. Therefore, our not seeing it doesn't equate to God not being able to bring it to pass.

Secondly, we are hesitant because we think that if God *can* do it, it may be less likely that He can do it with *us*. Knowing our shortcomings, there is a good chance that God's plan couldn't be carried out with *our* hands. We highlight the areas that clearly disqualify us from being considered as a participant in the movement of God and find every reason to believe that the holy outcome and our shortcomings can't possibly be aligned.

Sometimes we would rather submit a list of more suitable candidates that should be considered for the assignment instead of answer it ourselves. But heaven keeps calling us. We even provide reasons and rationales for why we should be further down on the "depth chart" of heaven's list of candidates. But heaven keeps calling us. Is God blind? Does heaven not see our dysfunction or incapacity? Why does heaven insist on calling us? In our human estimation, such a wise God should clearly know that there are more suitable candidates for the assignment.

Though such a thought process may seem to be a logical conclusion, it is not a very biblical one. Biblically, God has a habit of calling the underqualified to pursue His greatest movements on earth. Noah saved the world but had a drinking problem. David was anointed King but wasn't kingly enough to be considered for the position by his own father. Peter was called to follow Jesus even after being a self-confessed "sinful" man.

Yet God worked mightily through each one.

Though there may have been a question of calling competency on the front end, there was no question about the completion of the calling on the back end. Noah built the ark, David became the greatest king in the history of Israel, and Peter was known as the leader of the disciples.

Your Name is Already on It • 30

What does this mean? It means that God isn't calling you to complete the outcome of the calling. God is calling you because He has already completed the outcome of the calling. You may not know it, but God had already created the strategy before He formed you in the womb. The calculations were already made and the qualifications listed. You didn't "make the cut." You were specifically designed for this. Even the rough edges of your earlier stages were customized nuances required for you to partner with God in bringing the calling to pass.

This movement was made with you in mind. It's already been done in heaven; you just haven't seen it completed on earth.

So instead of shrinking back, move forward knowing that the calling has been waiting on you. It wasn't meant to be released to anyone else. IT WAS RESERVED FOR YOU. And now that you are here, it can come to pass.

Therefore, instead of choosing against God, choose with God. Trust God's choice more than you trust your own knowledge of your personal history. Though you may not be certain on the why, lean into God's selection of the "who." Know that God's plan will unfold in a way that may not be evident today but will prove to work in the end. Rest in the assurance that God has worked the end result out, even before you started the job.

Winning the War Within:
Retrieving the Reserved Blessing
(An exercise for reflection)

What is REALLY making you doubt that God can give you what He is promising?

_____
_____
_____
_____

What do you own that, at one point in your life, you never thought you'd own?

_____
_____
_____

Where have you been that, in earlier years, you never thought you would go?

_____
_____
_____

What would you say to the younger version of yourself who would have doubted being able to own those things and travel to those places?

_____

_____

_____

_____

_____

How does that statement speak to your life in this season of nervousness?

_____

_____

_____

_____

Statement of Affirmation:

If God is showing it to me, He has already secured it for me.

Prayer of Courage:

Heavenly Father, give me the grace to pursue every promise You have placed before me with the peace of knowing You have already reserved it for me. In Jesus' name, I ask this, AMEN.

PROCEED

Hearing from the LORD
(THIRTY MINUTES OF SILENT REFLECTION):

What is the LORD saying about how He has secured the promise, which lies ahead of you?

_____

_____

_____

_____

_____

_____

_____

_____

_____

_____

_____

_____

_____

_____

_____

GOD'S GOT YOU COVERED

As I was with Moses, so I will be with you;
I will not fail you or forsake you.

– Joshua 1:5 *NRSV*

The most vivid memory of my earliest days of driving was the day after I successfully passed the driving test and received my license. I was so happy to officially be able to drive; but beneath the surface, I was worried about getting into a car accident. Days later, my mother came to me with a card in her hand. She presented it and informed me she had added me to her auto insurance policy. It brought me great comfort to know as I was driving, the same insurance agency covering my mother would be with me as well. No longer did I have anything to fear because I knew there was no driver on the road – and no unfortunate event I would face – which the insurance company couldn't handle.

Joshua's concern wasn't so much about the promised land as it was about its inhabitants. The Canaanites, Hittites, Perizzites, Jebusites, Amorites and Hivites were already inhabiting the land and posed a significant military obstacle to secure the land. Therefore, the LORD assured Joshua he would have divine protection and offensive aid in the same manner as his predecessor, Moses. Joshua witnessed God provide success in the battles against the kings Sihon and Og in the wilderness of Moab. Now, that same supernatural might was promised to Joshua as he would face the awaiting enemies in pursuit of the land of Canaan.

Many of us as leaders get nervous about what's ahead because we wonder if our resources are enough to give us the victory promised by the LORD. It is in these moments the LORD reminds us we are not being "sent" into the promise; we are being "ushered" into the promise. God will not fail us, nor forsake us before, during or after the battles we face. Think about it: The All-Powerful, Sovereign, Victorious God of all creation is with you as you move forward in pursuit. Go in confidence, for you will be successful because you aren't going alone.

THE**UPGRADE:**
COMMUNION

Will I find spiritual communion with God sweet enough, and hope in His promises deep enough, not just to cope, but to flourish and rejoice in Him?

– John Piper, *A Hunger for God*

One of the greatest mistakes we can make when receiving a divine calling is to assume that God gives us the opportunity and we must accomplish it on our own. We can think that like a letter or package, God delivers the invitation and walks away from the moment leaving us to figure out how to bring it to pass. This is why many of us choose to deny the calling. We look at our strengths and weaknesses and attempt to gauge whether or not *we* can make it happen. Upon noticing that our skills and giftings do not provide the sufficient resources to achieve what we are being called to do, we compare God's plan and our proficiency and conclude that the only possible outcome would be to fumble the assignment or fail in it.

I want to provide another perspective that will hopefully assist you in re-wiring your understanding of how callings are presented and the Divine heart with which they are presented. When callings come to us, we have already discovered that God is fully aware of what we do and don't have in our skillset. So why would God entrust us with a calling that is beyond our capacity to handle? The answer is found when we shift our attention from the invitation to the Inviter.

Consider the fact that God is hand-delivering the invitation to you, not dropping it off with you. God brings the callings to us to remind us that we aren't only receiving the assignment, but that we are being introduced to the assignment *and* the Assigner. In essence, God is not handing the assignment to us; He is presenting an opportunity to carry out the assignment with Him.

Though you may be the face people see and the one who has to "talk to Pharoah," you are actually intended to be the co-star of the assignment. You're receiving an invitation to stewardship, not ownership. God never intended to take His hand off the mission, He is just inviting your hands to be on it as well. It's God saying, "I am going to do it, and I am going to give you the privilege of being in it with me." (Eims, 1975)

It is this fellowship that will make the difference in how the calling is not only performed, but also how it will be pursued. The moment of invitation is intended to be an offer to participate in a fellowship that will guide you into a "God-discovery" designed to introduce you to the Power of possibility.

This fellowship will aid us in uncovering three core truths that will grow us in new ways as we witness the vision of God become a reality. The journey with God is intended to reveal: 1) what God brings to our lives; 2) why our vulnerability is significant for the holy fellowship; and 3) how our communion is the key to our successful finishing.

The first element of this fellowship with God is that we realize what God brings to our lives. Each of our callings are divinely designed to exceed whatever level of competence we bring to the table. The assignment comes with a "God-gap." God built it with His own competence in mind. God knows who He is and creates the calling so that when our ability falls short, He can reveal His character and nature to us. This foreseen revealing is why He calls us.

God plans on being able to show you that He can part the "Red Sea" that lies between you and the promise. However, such revelation is only given after you have the confidence to be obedient to the farthest extent of your ability. It's why God didn't reveal the lamb caught in the thicket until Abraham raises his hand to slay his son or Peter doesn't learn to walk on water until he gets out of the boat. Know that when you will trust him with all that you can do, God remains with you in the calling to show you what He will add to your obedience to produce extraordinary outcomes. In short, if you are obedient in performing the "natural", God plans to add the "super"; and you will witness the supernatural come to pass.

The second element of this fellowship with God is to expose us to our own weakness and introduce us to a life of vulnerability before God. God doesn't desire an equal. He desires a person who will submit to His plan knowing that without God, it cannot come to pass. Communion with God is never meant to make us feel insignificant, but it is designed to show us that we are not self-sufficient. As the LORD walks with us and we commune with Him, every conversation informs us that God's vision, knowledge and ability far exceeds our own. However, this understanding of God is to show us our own weakness, so that we will always lean into His strength.

As LeRoy Eims states in his book, *Be the Leader You Were Meant to Be*, "God brings about a spirit of excellence in us by helping us realize our own weaknesses." (Eims, 1975) Our vulnerability allows us to see that our greatest pursuits will only become accomplished with the strength of Jesus. Such an understanding gives us a freedom to not have to be perfect, have all the answers or take on the pressure of completing the assignment with what's "in our bag." We have a God that accepts that we may stutter, not have a high IQ, or be cast out by the crowd, yet still allows us to complete assignments that will far exceed what we ever thought we could see done with our hands.

This leads to the final element of fellowship with God. It is designed to remind us of the necessity of communion with God on a regular basis. In these spaces of prayer, we gain the information, inspiration and impartation needed to fulfill the calling with accuracy and efficiency.

I used to always (and still do) get frustrated driving behind student drivers. They seem to always find a way to be in my lane of traffic, going slower than the speed limit. They would take forever to turn and never seem to look in the rear-view mirror and notice the growing line of traffic following them. This frustration was lessened (to some small degree) when I actually took the time to look into one of the student driver cars. It dawned on me that their slow driving was not the result of negligence, but attentiveness to the directives of the instructor with them. They were humbling themselves to guarantee that they would make it to their destination in a manner that was commensurate with the instructor's plan.

This is how our assignments are given. God invites us into the driver's seat with the hope that we will not try to control the trip but, instead, progress with humility knowing that our success will be in our listening more than our knowing. To be effective in the calling, you have to find a way to cultivate an ability to not rush to the destination and miss the voice of the One who is "riding" with you.

Refuse to think that you are more knowledgeable because of your "seat in the car." Know that you were invited and this journey with God will require constant communion to make it to the destination. Through this communion you will discover the All-Surpassing Power of the God with you. As Bill Perkins states, "The more time you spend with God the better you'll know him; the better you know him the more you'll trust him; the more you trust him the more you'll tap into his power." (Perkins, 2000)

Winning the War Within:
The LORD Is with You!
(An exercise for reflection)

What is ahead of you that makes you nervous about moving forward?

_____

_____

_____

_____

_____

Read these promises from God. Which of them can be used to offset your fear?

Romans 8:31
Joshua 10:42
Psalm 56:4
Isaiah 54:17
Jeremiah 1:19
1 John 4:4

_____

_____

_____

_____

How does God being with you make the difference in the outcome?

_____

_____

_____

_____

_____

Statement of Affirmation:

The LORD won't invite me to anything He won't see me through.

Prayer of Courage:

Heavenly Father, thank you for being with me. Grant me the grace to be ever mindful of Your presence and power as I pursue the vision you have given. In Jesus' name, I ask this, AMEN.

Hearing from the LORD
(THIRTY MINUTES OF SILENT REFLECTION):

What is the LORD saying concerning His commitment to your protection in the journey ahead?

YOU'LL NEED COURAGE AND COMPLIANCE

*Be strong and courageous; for you shall put
this people in possession of the land that I swore
to their ancestors to give them. Only be strong and
very courageous, being careful to act in accordance
with all the law that my servant Moses commanded
you; do not turn from it to the right hand or to
the left, so that you may be successful wherever
you go. This book of the law shall not depart out
of your mouth; you shall meditate on it day and night,
so that you may be careful to act in accordance
with all that is written in it. For then you shall make
your way prosperous, and then you shall be successful.*

– Joshua 1:6-8 NRSV

A few years back, I took swimming lessons. The only part of the lessons I remember was when the instructor looked at me and said, "Now it's your turn. Go for it!" I remember looking back at him and thinking, "I quit." It dawned on me: though I had received lessons in the mechanics of swimming, mental competence didn't ensure guaranteed success if there was no willingness to swim. Swimming required that I have courage to leave the security of the shallow waters and step into a less "safe" area of the pool. Then the instructor made a statement I'll never forget, "Just do what I taught you and you'll be fine." He was letting me know everything I needed to be successful had already been given to me, if I was willing to remember and follow it.

In a similar manner, God gave Joshua the final emotional push into the deep waters of his calling. The LORD understood no calling can be completed if it isn't pursued with confidence. The sidelines of major ministry movements are littered with souls of people who lacked the hunger and initiative to advance, despite the challenges before them. God wanted to make sure Joshua didn't miscarry his ministry by reminding him of the keys of calling success: confidence and compliance.

The calling to conquer the Promised Land would require a measure of audacity and ability, which would provide the endurance to not resign until the assignment was completed and the Israelites possessed the land. Secondly, the conquest would require Joshua to align his life and directives with the law of Moses. The law of God would have to be the primary strategy for camp operation and vision implementation. It was to be the non-negotiable truth by which every decision would be measured and gauged. If Joshua could do these two things, he was destined for prosperity and success.

As leaders, it is imperative we consider whether or not we are operating with these two elements at the forefront of our pursuit of the assignment we have been given. God can give you the calling, but you have to supply the courage and the compliance. Are you pursuing the calling with strength and courage, or are you approaching it with fear and hesitation? Are you allowing the Bible to be your primary manual for strategy, or is it your secondary source of guidance? If we are to be successful and prosperous in our callings, it will begin when we shift our disposition to one of courage and our devotion to the Word of God.

THE UPGRADE:
COURAGE

The weak persist only when things go their way.
The strong persist and pursue through discouragement,
deception and even abandonment. Pertinacity is often
the key to achieving difficult assignments
or meeting challenging goals.

– Wess Roberts,
Leadership Secrets of Attila the Hun

There are many resources that God can provide to assist us in the accomplishing of the calling upon our lives. But there is one thing that He prevents Himself from giving us that is central to finding success in the calling. That resource is the character trait of courage. Courage is the ability to be fearless and have the fortitude to carry out the assignments given…the gallantry to accept the risks of leadership. "Those with courage must not balk at the sight of obstacles, nor must they become bewildered when in the presence of adversity." (Roberts, 1987)

Courage is something that *we* have to both summon and sustain. It cannot be borrowed from another person, nor deposited by heaven. It must come from *us*. Interestingly enough, every major calling comes on the holy knowledge of our ability to produce courage. This is where God exercises His greatest faith in us. He believes that if we are invited to the calling, regardless of how timid we may be at the outset, something inside of us will discover a way to harness the courage needed to "take a shot" with God.

As you are reading this book, you may be wondering how to get the courage to pursue something that is clearly beyond your human ability to conquer. Every measurement taken of what lies ahead of you affirms the fact that you have not over-estimated its reality. IT'S BIG. So how do you gain the fortitude to muster courage to move forward? Courage is born of three personal affirmations that will give you permission to "square your shoulders" and proceed.

The first affirmation is, "IT IS BIG...TODAY." This affirmation allows you to rest in the fact that you have measured accurately and seen it clearly. However, the measurement only looks that way today.

I'll never forget taking a trip back to my elementary school a few years ago and seeing the stair rail I used to slide down as a third grader. I visited the playground and blacktop that I enjoyed for so many recess periods. Upon examination, I noticed something: they were so much smaller than I remembered. The fact is that they hadn't changed in size, I had grown up.

Take a moment and think about things that were big to you as a kid, but seem to have gotten so much smaller as you have aged. These things serve to provide a subtle reminder that things that look big in one stage of life will seem smaller in later stages of growth and development. This is the first secret to gaining courage. It is understanding that *it only looks large to me because of my faith, hope and view today.* However, as I begin to believe the plan and power of God at higher levels, then I will see it as He sees it. And that growth will never happen if I don't choose to follow God into pursuing it. As I learn, develop and "grow up", it will begin to appear less daunting and unachievable.

The second courage-inspiring affirmation is, "IT IS BIG...BUT GOD IS BIGGER." When receiving a calling from God, we must always remember that God had already seen the result before we began the path. God had already completed the entire success plan before making the offer to you. This means that God has already determined how what is in front of you will be conquered effectively.

God's certainty in success is an indication that the challenge before you is within His ability to easily overcome. In other words, God is BIGGER. God is not concerned with *whether* His plan will work. He's *already* seen it work and is calling you to witness it for yourself.

When you understand that God is not calling you to an assignment He has yet to "figure out," you can know that having God with you must clearly be greater than what is in front of you. Our courage is not summoned on our potential, but on His. We move with absolute confidence that God is going to make it happen regardless of the size of the challenges before us. If God is going to make it happen, then we must have the courage to move forward.

The third affirmation that we must embrace if we are to move courageously is, "IT IS BIG...AND MAY STILL FAIL." Our greatest enemy to courage is the rehearsal of the history of the obstacle before us. Many times, we dismiss our courage because we have reviewed the past performance of the challenge before us. We pay attention to the carcasses of competitors who have tried and failed to overcome the same obstacle in the past and assume that their fortune is our forecast.

In these moments, we must shift our attention from their past record to the successful record of the God who is with us. God remains undisputed and undefeated in every conquest and plan. He is still all-powerful and sovereign and that's not about to change any time soon.

The key to success is our ability to trust God enough to follow His strategy even when it doesn't seem to make sense. Whether God is telling you to throw a rock at a giant or touch the edge of a garment to stop a twelve-year flow of blood, somehow God has a history of making it end in victory.

This moment is no different. THIS WILL END IN A "GOD-VICTORY". If you are willing to move forward courageously, you will witness another unusual outcome and walk away having seen what looked like a certain tragedy produce an unmistakable testimony.

Winning the War Within:
Gaining Your Courage
(An exercise for reflection)

In his book, *The Magic of Thinking Big,* David Schwartz states, "Action cures fear." (Schwartz, 1987)

Which outcomes do you fear may happen if you pursue the calling right now?

_____

_____

_____

_____

_____

_____

What are three actions you can take to begin to pursue your calling?

_____

_____

_____

_____

_____

_____

When will you take them?

_____

_____

_____

_____

What's the worst that can happen? Is the negative outcome reversible?

_____

_____

_____

_____

What's the best that can happen? Who would benefit from it?

_____

_____

_____

_____

If you move forward according to the Word of God, what does the LORD promise? (What did He promise Joshua?)

_____

_____

_____

_____

Statement of Affirmation:

If I can muster the courage and compliance, God will give the prosperity and success.

Prayer of Courage:

Heavenly Father, grant me the grace to have the courage to move forward and the humility to not move forward without your Word guiding me. In Jesus' name, I ask this, AMEN.

Hearing from the LORD
(THIRTY MINUTES OF SILENT REFLECTION):

What is the LORD saying to you about having the courage to move forward?

_____

_____

_____

_____

_____

_____

Where is the LORD directing you to be more devoted to His word as you proceed into the assignment?

_____

_____

_____

_____

_____

_____

COMMUNICATE WITH CONFIDENCE

Then Joshua commanded the officers of the people,
"Pass through the camp, and command the people:
'Prepare your provisions; for in three days you are to
cross over the Jordan, to go in to take possession of
the land that the Lord your God gives you to possess.'"

– Joshua 1:10-11 *NRSV*

Once Joshua had received the instruction of the LORD, he turned to those in the camp and told them to prepare to take possession of the land. Then he reminded them of the promised outcome reserved for them. Joshua understood the successful conquering of the land would require more than just him. It would require the assistance of those around him. However, the forward movement had to be communicated as more than just a bright idea. It had to be concrete and measurable.

He told them three things: prepare your provisions, we are leaving in three days, and we are going to take possession of the land. Do you hear how specific he was? There was no ambiguity or grey area for misinterpretation. He let the people know they were moving forward with the plan of God.

In his book, *The 17 Indisputable Laws of Teamwork*, John Maxwell introduces a concept he calls, "The Law of the Compass." He reminds us that "every team needs a compelling vision to give it direction." (Maxwell, 2001) Providing vision is more than showing a PowerPoint presentation or listing some bullet points on a sheet of paper. It is *embodying* the wherewithal to move forward with confidence. The sharing of vision should feel more like an invitation to join a relevant "why" than a presentation to listen to an objective "what." The specifics of the vision do just that. The details allow the listener to determine whether or not the plan placed before them fits their "why." It is when people are able to clearly see how the vision aligns with their own calling that you will notice a shift in their enthusiasm and willingness to participate in the plan laid before them. As Maxwell states, "...a team that embraces a vision becomes focused, energized, and confident." (Maxwell, 2001)

Everyone following you is waiting to be inspired to move forward. Though they may not always fully understand the strategy, people connected to leaders possess an inner yearning for the next move. Hesitation and stagnation never work in favor of the person appointed to lead. Therefore, it is not enough to be personally inspired if you aren't willing to translate that inspiration into the pursuit of your assignment and usher others toward the fulfillment of their God-given outcomes. Vision must ALWAYS connect to the passion and purpose of those working alongside you. Once they see how they fit into the vision and how the vision fits into their journeys, they discover and display a new sense of possible achievement and respond accordingly. You have to be intentional about expressing a personal commitment to moving forward and show them that it is not only going to happen but, with God, it will be successful.

In addition, communicating the assignment gives those following you an opportunity to hold you accountable to complete the calling. By expressing a commitment to begin, the team has an opportunity to assess the clear and present progress and provide feedback on the assignment. Though many leaders are hesitant to embrace correction, such feedback can be critical to your success. As stated in the Harvard Business Review's article, *6 Strategies for Leading Through Uncertainty*, "…we can exponentially expand our knowledge and perspective by cultivating and connecting with a network of peers and colleagues – each with their own set of experiences and perspectives." (Rowell, 2021) God places those alongside us into our circles for a reason. Leadership is not intended to only encourage an invitation to follow; it should also offer an invitation to healthy dialogue in moments of concern and uncertainty in the team. Those following you are not your enemies. They are your teammates and have been sent to provide insight in moments when the leader's vision may lack certain perspectives. By offering an opportunity for dialogue, you extend your peripheral view and will be able to gain levels of vision not attained in isolation.

Now is the time to step forward and let those with you know the days of passivity and complacency are over, and the days of forward movement have arrived! Lead with boldness and confidence as you fulfill the calling of God upon your life.

PROCEED

Winning the War Within:
It's Time to Move Forward!
(An exercise for reflection)

What do you need to put into place before moving forward in the calling?

_____
_____
_____
_____
_____
_____
_____

What roles do you need alongside you to effectively accomplish the vision?

_____
_____
_____
_____
_____
_____
_____

Have you created a description of responsibilities? How will creating these descriptions let them know you're serious about moving forward?

_____

_____

_____

_____

_____

What date can you give them as a launch date?

_____

_____

_____

_____

_____

What outcome can you communicate to them as a result of their work?

_____

_____

_____

_____

_____

Statement of Affirmation:

If you can believe the vision, God will send the team who can help you get the victory.

Prayer of Courage:

Heavenly Father, give me the grace to identify the team needed to carry out the assignment. Then provide me with the details needed to give them your plan and promise. In Jesus' name, I ask this, AMEN.

Hearing from the LORD
(THIRTY MINUTES OF SILENT REFLECTION):

What is the LORD telling you to communicate to those moving forward alongside you?

Communicate with Confidence • 69

Bibliography

Aurelius, M. (2002). *The Meditations.* New York: Random House.

Eims, L. (1975). *Be the Leader You Were Meant to Be: Biblical Principles of Leadership.* Wheaton, IL: Victor Books.

Goleman, D. (1995). *Emotional Intelligence: Why it can matter more than IQ.* New York: Bantam Books.

Maxwell, J. (2001). *17 Indisputable Laws of Teamwork: Embrace them and empower your team.* Nashville: Thomas Nelson.

Perkins, B. (2000). *Awaken the Leader Within: How the Wisdom of Jesus Can Unleash Your Potential.* Grand Rapids: Zondervan.

Piper, J. (1997). *A Hunger for God: Desiring God through Fasting and Prayer.* Wheaton: Crossway.

Roberts, W. (1987). *Leadership Secrets of Attila the Hun.* New York: Warner Books.

Rowell, R. Z. (2021, April 26). *6 Strategies for Leading Through Uncertainty.* Retrieved from Harard Buisness Review: https://hbr.org/2021/04/6-strategies-for-leading-through-uncertainty

Santos-Longhurst, A. (2019, February 5). Nervousness: How You Can Deal with It and Feel Better. Retrieved from Healthline: https://www.healthline.com/health/anxiety/nervousness

Schwartz, D. J. (1987). *The Magic of Thinking Big.* New York: Simon & Schuster.

Seaver, M. (2020, February 05). *The Top 5 Reasons for New Job Jitters, and How to Stay Calm Before Your First Day.* Retrieved from Real Simple: https://www.realsimple.com/work-life/life-strategies/job-career/nervous-about-new-job

Shakespeare, W. (1992). *The Tragedy of Hamlet, Prince of Denmark.* New York: Washington Square Press/Pocket Books.